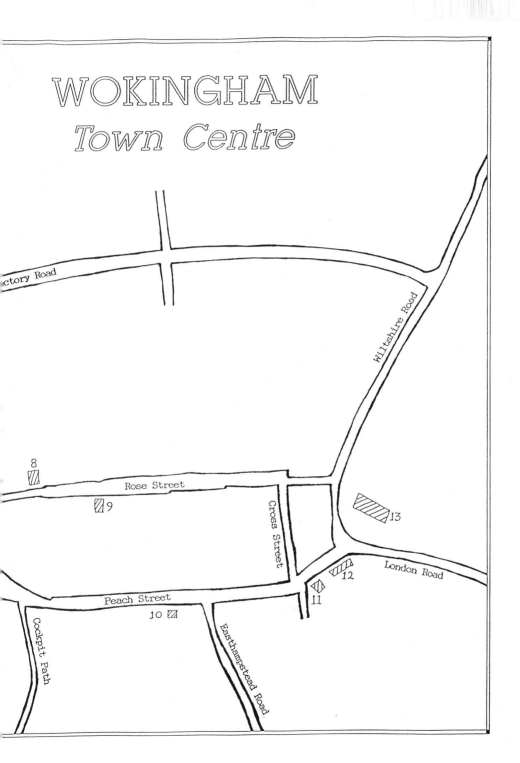

WOKINGHAM
Town Centre

...ctory Road

Wiltshire Road

8

Rose Street

9

Cross Street

13

London Road

12

11

Peach Street

10

Cockpit Path

Easthampstead Road

WOKINGHAM
A Pictorial History

The Terrace from Station Road

WOKINGHAM
A Pictorial History

John and
Rosemary Lea

Phillimore

1990

Published by
PHILLIMORE & CO. LTD
Shopwyke Hall, Chichester, Sussex

ISBN 0 85033 748 8

Printed and bound in Great Britain by
BIDDLES LTD.,
Guildford, Surrey

List of Illustrations

Acknowledgements

This book is the result of the collective efforts of the History Group of the Wokingham Society. On its behalf, we would like to thank Glen Stewart; the Wokingham Society; Studio Carr of Wokingham; Colin Farnell; Ken Goatley; and the Museum of English Rural Life, Reading University, for permission to use photographs from their collections.

We are also indebted to Dennis Ayres, Roger Hosking and Pauline Tate for their help with the selection of photographs and the editing of the captions. Particular thanks are due to Dennis for his work on the introduction.

Finally, we must thank Ken and Edna Goatley and Meg Goswell, whose families have long connections with Wokingham, for their invaluable advice.

Introduction

Wokingham cannot claim an entry in Domesday Book, but it has a long history and has Royal Charters from 1219 giving it the right to hold a market every week. For centuries it was a small market town which remained virtually unchanged until the 20th century. By the middle of the 19th century it had a population of less than 4,000 and served a mainly agricultural community. Maps of Wokingham at this period show a market place and five principal roads.

At the present time Wokingham is going through a period of change unparalleled in its history. During the last 20 years the town has expanded at a much faster rate than ever before. It has ceased to be a quiet country town and is now a thriving centre for business and light industry. Despite all this change the basic layout of the historic centre of the town remains unaltered and 20th-century Wokingham still boasts a market place and the same five main roads: Peach Street, Denmark Street, Broad Street, Rose Street and Shute End. Most of the recent expansion of Wokingham has been outside the original boundary of the town, but a number of historic buildings in the centre have been demolished and replaced by modern structures.

The name Wokingham suggests that it began as a tiny Saxon settlement, but little else is known. The original settlement was probably not located in the present town centre, as the area was largely heathland of poor agricultural quality. There is no mention of Wokingham in Domesday Book, but the Manor of Sonning was recorded as belonging to the Bishop of Salisbury. This was a large estate which corresponded approximately with the present day District of Wokingham, of which the town of Wokingham is a part.

By the early 12th century a chapel of ease had been built, which was consecrated as All Saints about 1190 and became a church in the 15th century. In the mid-12th century the glebe land of the chapel was cleared and brought into cultivation. It became known as 'the clearing', a name which suggests that it stood out from the surrounding area of heath or scrub. A quirk of land ownership led to All Saints' church being built outside the boundary of the town, in a detached part of Wiltshire, no doubt because the owner of the land provided the money, built the chapel on his land and later gave it to the Bishop of Salisbury. The former line of Cross Street formed the boundary between Berkshire and Wiltshire and was also part of the boundary of the town of Wokingham. It was marked by a stone, which was later moved to its present site on the corner of Rose Street and Wiltshire Road.

In the early 13th century the population was large enough for the Bishop of Salisbury to administer the area of Wokingham town as a separate manor. In the second decade of that century, together with the Dean of Salisbury, he founded the town proper. They set out burgage plots along the existing roads or tracks. These were mostly about one-tenth of an acre in area and were made available to all free men for a rent of about one shilling per year. Around the same time the bishop bought from the Crown the right to hold a market in his town and to collect the tolls from it. In 1258 he also bought the right to hold three fairs a year there. Before the end of the century Wokingham had become recognised as a town for legal purposes.

The early 14th-century town consisted of only six or seven streets. These were Rose

Street, Peach Street, Denmark Street, Market Place, Broad Street, The Terrace and possibly a small part of Milton Road, then unnamed. Rose Street is the first street of which there is any known record. Although the very earliest buildings have all fallen down, or were pulled down long ago, the layout of the street has been preserved. It is a rare surviving example of an enclosed medieval street. It was originally called Le Rothe Street, that is the Street of the Clearing or Clearing Street. The Terrace was called La Schete, from which comes the present-day Shute End; otherwise it was known by the descriptive name of High Street. Denmark Street was called Le Don Street, later Down Street, meaning Hill Street. It retained this name until 1865, when it was renamed Denmark Street in honour of the Princess of Denmark who later became Queen Alexandra. Broad Street appears to have been the last street to be developed as it did not have a name until the middle of the 14th century when, together with The Terrace, it began to be called High Street.

Most people in the medieval town earned their living from agriculture, although the quality of the land in the district restricted the amount of arable farming. The major emphasis was on pastoral farming, mainly rearing horses, cattle and sheep, together with the consequent trades of tanning leather and producing and weaving wool. This set the pattern for many centuries until the advent of cheap lime and fertilisers and attention to land drainage made it more profitable to grow arable crops.

A unique aspect of the early town was the bell foundry, which started in the early 14th century and, in one form or another, existed for the next 300 years. It seems to have been started by a bell founder who had been trained in London and then moved into the area. Although the early bells were not very good, by the second half of the 14th century they were of the highest quality. For most of the 15th century, when the foundry was owned by the Landen family, a substantial proportion of the church bells in southern England was made in Wokingham. Some have been found in places as far away as Peterborough and Somerset. In the 1490s most of the industry moved to Reading but a small number of bells continued to be made in Wokingham. The industry was given a new lease of life in 1564 when it was taken over by the Eldridge family, and it continued to thrive until about 1620 when it was finally moved to Chertsey. Only the site of the 15th-century and later foundry is known. It was behind a house in Broad Street called Smyth's Place, which for obvious reasons became known as the Bellhouse. The exact site has not been identified, but it is known to have been somewhere behind what are now Nos. 7 to 13 Broad Street. Bronze slag has been found in a pit on the land behind No. 7.

The 15th century was a time of comparative prosperity for Wokingham, quite unlike the situation in the greater part of England, where many towns decayed. It was a time when many of the oldest surviving buildings of Wokingham were built, particularly those in Rose Street. Although of 15th-century origin, few look old because over the centuries their external appearance has been radically changed.

Also from the 15th century comes the first mention of the Alderman of Wokingham, the leader of the administration of the town. The Alderman is not mentioned in the early charters bought by the Bishop of Salisbury, and the first official mention is to be found in the Charter of Queen Elizabeth I of 1583. This form of local government continued throughout the 17th, 18th and most of the 19th centuries, with representatives of the richer families in the town taking turns to be the Alderman.

Although Wokingham seems to have been a prosperous town in the early 17th century, it was badly affected by the Civil War. In 1643-4 the district was the centre of an area subject to foraging raids by both the Roundheads and the Cavaliers. The latter raided the town on market days to seize horses for their cavalry and on one occasion sent as many as 80 carts to take away their loot. At least twice, the Cavaliers set fire to houses in Wokingham in reprisal for the failure of the inhabitants to supply enough food for their forces in Reading. Thirty or more houses are known to have been burnt down, about 20 per cent of the town at that time.

The town only slowly recovered from the effects of the war. Even 15 years after the wars had ended, about 20 per cent of the town's house owners were too poor to pay the Hearth Tax. Perhaps the poverty of Wokingham at that time was a consideration that in 1663 led Henry Lucas to build his 'Hospital' for 16 poor single men close to the town. Today it accepts married couples and can be seen at Chapel Green, east of the Reading to Guildford railway line and a few hundred yards beyond the end of Luckley Road. After three centuries it is still a magnificent building, the only Grade I listed building in Wokingham.

For most of the 18th century Wokingham was a relatively prosperous town. This and the fashion for houses of brick led to many of the 15th- and 16th-century houses being given a shell of brick. Sometimes, as in the case of The Elms in Broad Street, the original timber-framed house was completely surrounded by a new brick building. Others, such as No. 25 The Terrace, were surrounded by a shell of brick to give the 15th-century house the appearance of one in the Georgian style. The most popular course of action was to add a brick front to the house. Several houses in Rose Street, and the old Heelas building in Market Place, were given this treatment.

Apart from agriculture and its supporting trades, there were a number of other industries in the town, although on a very small scale. From very early times the production of wool led to the trades of weaving and wool sorting. Weaving had virtually ended by the close of the 18th century, unable to compete with the large-scale factory production in the north of England, but wool sorting continued well into the 19th century. Malt was produced to sell to the recently evolved brewing industry in London. The *Red Lion* is a reminder of this, being the only building in Wokingham known to have been a malt house.

Overall, the 18th century was probably the town's most prosperous period before the present day. The traditional industries were still active and, in addition, for some years a newspaper was published in the town, a stage coach ran to London (two ran for a few years) and there was a silk industry from 1771 onwards. The town was prosperous enough to be regularly visited by companies of travelling actors. Many of Wokingham's finest buildings date from this time; The Elms, Colbourne House, and Montague House (rebuilt about 1803) are good examples. However, all was changed by the time of the onset of the Napoleonic Wars.

From about 1790, through the Napoleonic Wars and up to the end of the second decade of the 19th century, Wokingham was a depressed area. After that it depended almost entirely for its livelihood on agriculture and the leather trades. The only other industry was shoe making. Attendances at the town market had been declining throughout the 18th and 19th centuries, and the fairs were also poorly attended in spite of efforts made by the Town Corporation to attract more trade. One by one they fell into disuse and were abandoned.

Despite the depression, the silk industry flourished until the 1820s, although wages were very low. Increased competition from France then led to its decline and the last silk factory closed in 1831. Until 1980 this still stood in South Place off Peach Street, although long since converted to cottages. Two of the former silk mills were taken over for wool sorting, the one in South Place being associated with the largest trader, James Twycross, who had other branches in Bradford and Rochdale, and in Melbourne, Australia.

At the beginning of the 19th century the population of the town was still small, about 1,400. At that time Wokingham was a quiet country town, but during the course of the century it was influenced by the coming of the railway, changes in local industry and the actions of one of the important local families, the Walters. The flourishing stage coach service that now ran between Reading and London through Wokingham continued until the middle of the century. It was largely superseded when the Reading to Guildford railway was built, since this allowed passengers to travel by rail to London via Reading. It was not heard of after 1856, when the rail connection from Staines to Reading provided a direct service to London.

In 1849 the railway from Guildford to Reading via Wokingham was completed. Wokingham station was sited a few minutes' walk away from the town centre. Within a few years the presence of the railway station led to substantial development of the surrounding area. The *Molly Millar*, originally the *Station Hotel*, dates from this time. The railway line itself was not a great financial success but it provided the inhabitants of Wokingham with an indirect connection to most parts of the country. Greater benefits came from the connection with Staines, and hence London. This was of great importance for the growth of the town and over the next half century led to the development of numerous small industries.

Formerly leather was produced at many sites around the town, most of them near the Embrook. The whereabouts of only three sites are known; one near the *Duke's Head*, one by the *Pin and Bowl* and one at Tan House Lane, off the Barkham Road. The two first named had ceased to make leather by the early 19th century, but production continued at the Tan House Lane site until about 1920. The main building was on the north side of the lane with the others set out along the stream. All have now gone and only photographic records remain.

From the middle of the 19th century a small industrial site grew up on the Embrook near the *Rifle Volunteer*. There was a paper mill which burnt down in the early 20th century. Metal working began on the same site, which by the turn of the century had resulted in a small bicycle factory and an iron foundry operating there. The latter must have been quite small but survived until the 1920s, when it was burnt down one Saturday afternoon. Little is known about it apart from two examples of its work: a manhole cover in Red Lion Path and the baker's oven in Blake's Lock museum in Reading.

After the coming of the railway to Wokingham the local brickmaking industry began to expand, since the railway provided easy transport for heavy materials over long distances. The raw materials were abundant in the area and the industry prospered and survived until ended by the 1939-45 war. One of the brickfields was at the station end of Oxford Road, where part of the site can still be seen. Not far away was the largest local brickfield. This was in what is now the Mulberry Business Park off Fishponds Road, the legendary Blue Pool site, which for many years had its own railway track crossing Molly Millars Lane and connected to the railway line near Wokingham station.

In earlier times inns and alehouses brewed their own beer. Only in the latter half of the 18th century did the concentration of pub ownership into a few hands allow the growth of breweries which supplied their beer to many pubs. The first Wokingham brewery of any size was owned by James Webb and was at Beches Manor in the Reading Road. The brewhouse was on the site of the present Masonic Hall. By 1820 the brewery was owned by James Hayward, whose family lived in Beches Manor. The house was later turned into an hotel before being burned down in 1953.

By the 1850s the Hayward Brewery had run into financial difficulties and was sold. Its collapse allowed two other breweries to develop: Baker's Brewery, behind what is now No. 15 Broad Street, and the Wellington Brewery on a site now occupied by Tesco's in Denmark Street. The latter obtained its water from a well that reached into the chalk 300 ft. below ground. Both breweries ceased production early in the present century: Baker's in 1915 after it had been bought by Brakspear's; and the Wellington Brewery, then owned by the Headington family, when it was bought and closed by Ashby's Brewery in 1920. All the buildings have since been demolished, those of the Wellington Brewery as recently as 1979.

In 1847 the Wokingham Gas Company started business, on a site off the Finchampstead Road, along Carey Road. By 1900 many houses in Wokingham had a gas supply, and gas was also used to light some of the town's streets.

The most important family in Wokingham in the 19th century was the Walter family, who owned the *Times* newspaper and who lived at Bearwood. John Walter III was an M.P. for many years. His actions had an enormous effect on the life of the town and many prominent memorials to his activities can still be seen in Wokingham today. During the 1850s and 1860s he bought a large area of land to the south of Wokingham and around Bearwood. Following the example of his father, who built St Catherine's church at Sindlesham in 1846, he built and endowed St Paul's church at his own expense. Today the church looks very much as it did when he had completed it in 1864. He later built St Paul's rectory, which is now the older part of the newly extended offices of the Wokingham District Council. By the early 1870s he had pulled down the old house at Bearwood that his father had erected and had built a replacement to his own design.

He made substantial changes in the surrounding countryside as well as in the town. One of the landmarks of the district today is Wellingtonia Avenue, a few miles south of Wokingham, near Finchampstead. This was a new road that he built through the Finchampstead Ridges about 1870 to provide a direct connection between Finchampstead and Sandhurst. He planted a row of Wellingtonia sequoia trees on either side of the road as a tribute to the Duke of Wellington. It is only in this century, as the trees begin to reach their full height, that the grandeur of his ideas can be properly appreciated.

During the closing decades of the 19th century he and his son, Arthur, built St Paul's Elementary School, Parish Room and Clock Tower on the Reading Road, just outside the former boundary of the town. In 1881 Arthur also built the Drill Hall in Denmark Street, which up to the 1970s was used for many town functions and as the headquarters for the Territorial Army.

The 19th century also saw the erection of several other churches in Wokingham. The Baptist chapel in Milton Road, which had existed since 1773, was enlarged in 1827. St Sebastian's church on Nine Mile Ride was built primarily for the broom makers of the area, initially in 1864 as a chapel of ease, becoming a full church with its own parish within a few years. In 1870 the Wesleyan Methodist church in Rose Street was built on the site of an earlier chapel that had been there since 1820. The Roman Catholic church on The Terrace was consecrated in 1911. This was subsequently sold and the new Corpus Christi Catholic church constructed and consecrated in Sturges Road in 1970.

The first substantial redevelopment of the town took place about 1842. The shops in Peach Street, centred around the *Redan* public house, were built on a site that extended to Rose Street. The part of this area reached from Rose Street became Chubbs Row, though it was later renamed Queen's Terrace. It consisted of a line of tiny low-cost houses with minimal facilities. A little later the ground in Reading Road was drained and land at Shute End was landscaped and embanked, which led to The Terrace receiving its present name.

In 1850 a new workhouse was built for the Wokingham Union, roughly the present Wokingham District, replacing the old house in Denmark Street that for two centuries had served as the workhouse. In 1858 the old Town Hall was pulled down and the Berkshire county authorities replaced it in 1860 by the present building in sham Gothic style. The old timber-framed Town Hall had been built about the end of the 16th century, originally with a thatched roof, and was in a poor condition. Less than 40 years earlier, in 1819, it had needed to be substantially rebuilt. The Wokingham Corporation, with an income of less than £50 a year, could only organise a public subscription to help pay for it. Until Wokingham became a borough, in 1885, the new Town Hall was largely used by the county. The present shops on the north side were originally police cells and were later converted to a fire station. When the first motor fire engine was bought by public subscription in 1912 it was kept there after the cells had been moved to the new police station in Rectory Road.

Next to the Town Hall, on the site which the market now occupies, bull baiting took place once a year, immediately before Christmas. Under the terms of the will of George Staverton, a butcher who died in 1661, two bulls were bought and baited in Market Place, tied up and attacked by dogs who tried to grip their muzzles. After they had been baited, the bulls were killed and the meat given to the poor of the town. The practice was a relic from the Middle Ages when it was thought unhealthy to eat the meat of a bull that had not been baited. By the end of the 18th century humanitarian voices were being raised against the practice, which was finally prohibited in 1821.

Throughout the 19th century the resources of the Wokingham Corporation had become more and more limited. It had neither the money nor the powers to administer the town, small though it was. It administered an area bounded by Cross Street, on the east, and the western end of The Terrace, on the west, extending from the bottom of Denmark Street to the end of Rose Street. The fairs and markets had almost fallen into disuse and there was a growing demand for Wokingham to have an elected council. In 1883 a town petition was organised which led to Wokingham becoming a borough in 1885. The Victorian charter gave the town an elected council for the first time in its long history. Wokingham was put under the control of a borough council responsible for a much greater area. This was enlarged in 1927 to take account of the expansion of the town. In 1974, when local government was reorganised throughout the country, Wokingham ceased to be a borough and became part of the District of Wokingham.

In the early part of the 20th century Wokingham continued its slow but steady expansion. The Sturges Road area was built before 1914. After a pause due to the 1914-18 war the town continued to expand slowly along and around the main roads: Reading Road, London Road, Barkham Road and Finchampstead Road. The first cinema opened about 1912 at No. 10 Broad Street and continued to run until the 1950s. A part-time county library service began in 1924, and in the following year electricity was brought to the town. Bus services started in the 1920s, almost 50 years later than in London. Unusual for its time, Martin's Pool was built by Councillor Martin as a private swimming pool and opened for public use in 1934. He had failed to convince his fellow councillors that the town needed a swimming pool and, as a result, built and operated one himself. It was not until 1946 that the borough council bought it .

After the Second World War Wokingham grew at a faster rate. Between 1948 and 1962 more than 750 council houses were built, almost as many as the total number of houses in the town at the beginning of the century. From the 1950s onwards private development was responsible for most of the house building. By the end of the 1980s housing estates had been built all round the town with the exception of the south-eastern sector. New housing has resulted in Wokingham now being joined to Winnersh and almost joined to California. The largest of the new estates, the Woosehill estate, is larger than the entire area of Wokingham at the beginning of the century.

Since 1945 changes in the industrial and social life of the country have brought about great changes in the trade and industry of the town. The industries of the later 19th century have been replaced by new light industries, particularly on the industrial estates on or near Molly Millars Lane. Industrial growth has been accompanied by a similar growth in office building, much of it located in the main streets of the town. The number of small shops began to decline after 1945 and today many small shops have been replaced by supermarkets, estate agencies and building societies. Some of the new offices and shops have been designed to fit in with old Wokingham, but some have not.

One unchanging aspect of the town is its large number of inns and public houses. No history of Wokingham would be complete without some mention of these institutions. At some time or other almost every house site in the centre of Wokingham has been occupied by some form of public house. Most existed for only a short time but some reverted to use as private houses, many of which survived until quite recently. Until the late 1970s there was a bakery on the corner of Rose Street and Broad Street. It is now the site of the National Westminster Bank, but in the early 1600s it was used as an inn called the *George*. Before the end of the 17th century it had ceased to trade and Wingmore Lodge, in Rose Street, was built on the site of its outbuildings. The *Bell Inn*, on the site now occupied by Milwards on the corner of Rose Street and Market Place, lasted for over 100 years before becoming a shop in the early 1700s. It was demolished in 1955. Bush Walk now occupies the site of the *Bush*, which was an inn until it was converted into a shopping arcade in 1988-9. It is a 15th- to 17th-century building, which was an inn before 1700 and one of the centres of town life in the 18th century. Stage coaches called regularly, and on one occasion Handel's oratorio 'Esther' was performed in the main hall. Next door to the *Bush* was the *Rose*, an even older inn, which probably started in late Tudor times. For a short period in the 18th century it was nationally famous because of the landlord's daughter, Molly Mogg, about whom Alexander Pope and his friends wrote a satirical ballad. For nearly one hundred years it was the centre of the stage coach trade in Wokingham and the main venue for important business. The governing bodies of the local turnpike trust, the local militia, the post and excise office all met there. In 1844 the *Rose* was closed down, but its licence and landlord moved across the road to the site of the present *Ye Olde Rose Inne*. There, for over a century, it was an hotel before becoming a Berni Inn in 1970. Sadly the 15th- to 16th-century building was almost destroyed by fire in the 1970s. It has been restored as closely as possible to the original structure and a few of the original beams can still be seen in the upper dining room.

Wokingham still has the *Red Lion* in Market Place, the *Queen's Head* on The Terrace, the *Lord Raglan*, the *Crispin* and the *Duke's Head* in Denmark Street, the *Ship* in Peach

Street and the *Metropolitan* in Rose Street, to name but a few, all of which are of historical interest and still flourishing.

Wokingham is no longer a quiet country town. It has become a busy centre for business and light industry, with many of its population commuting daily to London or to nearby Reading and Bracknell. Despite the expansion of the town, Wokingham is still a pleasant place in which to live and retains a certain charm and character.

It is hoped that this book, which sets out to show what the town was like in the past, will both bring back memories to the older inhabitants and provide newer residents with a glimpse of Wokingham in a quieter era.

1.   An early aerial view of the Market Place, taken about 1930. The two-way traffic in Peach Street and Denmark Street has now been replaced by a one-way system. Parking was no problem in these earlier days.

2. This 'Souvenir from Wokingham' was posted in the town on 23 October 1907.

3. This view of All Saints' church at the junction of London Road and Wiltshire Road was painted in 1832 by W. A. Delamott, drawing master at the Royal Military College at Sandhurst, when the church was on the very edge of the town. The rutted dirt roads and the relaxed figures show how different was the pace of life from that of today.

4. In the 1920s Wiltshire Road was still a quiet backwater; this photograph evokes the peace of that era.

5. Early Tudor cottages which once stood at the eastern end of Rose Street, with All Saints' church in the background. Notice that the dirt road had no pavement at the time this photograph was taken in 1890.

6. Rose Street viewed from Wiltshire Road in the 1970s. On the left of the photograph is a house which was once the *White Hart* public house and the home of the Rose family. On the corner, in Wiltshire Road, is the marker of the former Berkshire and Wiltshire border which was moved to this site from the south end of Cross Street.

7. The far end of Rose Street in about 1910, showing the Tudor cottages and the entrance to Cross Street. The road has now been surfaced and a footpath laid. The photograph clearly shows the closed end of Rose Street.

8. On the right hand side of this view of Rose Street can be seen the Methodist church, formerly the Wesleyan chapel. Isaiah Gadd had strong connections with the church, and he and his family lived at one time in St Mary's, the bow-fronted house opposite. The cottage on the right of the church was home to the caretaker.

9. The corner of Cross Street and Rose Street around 1895. The road had a dirt surface at that time.

10. Cross Street in the 1950s showing the 'prefabs' – temporary housing erected shortly after the Second World War on waste land that had once been the yards and workshop of J. Hopkins, the wheelwright's. Cross Street, once known as Rosemary Lane, formed part of the boundary of the medieval town and the county of Berkshire.

11. An artist's impression of the original state of Nos. 33-37 Rose Street. The windows would have been barred but without glass and would have had removable shutters. They were originally hall-houses and the smoke vents can be clearly seen on the roof, which would have been thatched or tiled.

L. d. V.

12.   No. 72 Rose Street, once the home of funeral director, Mr. Yalden, and his family. The hearse was housed behind the double doors on the right hand side. His daughter was for some time the organist at nearby All Saints' church. The flock of fantail pigeons was a feature of Rose Street in the 1960s.

13.   The landlord and his customers outside the *Metropolitan* public house in Rose Street, about 1900. The publican is wearing the bowler hat and shirt sleeves. The building is a 15th-century hall-house, modified over the centuries to meet the needs of its owners.

14. This picture of Rose Street was taken at the turn of the century. The man to the left of the pair on the right hand side of the road may be Isaiah Gadd, a local businessman who owned Wingmore Lodge at that time. They are standing outside one of his furniture depositories which have now been pulled down, though the houses opposite are still there.

15. Nos. 16-18 Rose Street are a 15th-century hall-house into which an upper floor was inserted in the 16th century. At the same time it was given a fireplace with chimneys and a fashionable overhung front. Shown here in 1925 as the business premises of F. Knight, plumber, it later became the soft furnishing and carpet business of C. and M. Ellen. In 1989 it was still a carpet shop.

16. A float in the Peace Day celebrations of 1919, passing down Rose Street.

17. Queen's Terrace, off Rose Street: a row of Victorian cottages with wash houses across the yard and toilets even further away. Originally named Chubb's Row, the terrace was demolished in the mid-1950s.

18. Two cottages in Rose Street that have now disappeared. They were replaced in 1965 by the Methodist centre for the church next door.

19.   These two buildings, photographed in about 1965, were the workshops for the Heelas store in Market Place. The opening provided rear access to both Heelas and the *Bush Hotel*. The site is now part of the car park in Rose Street.

20.   This picture, taken in 1965, shows Wingmore Lodge in Rose Street. This is a magnificent early 18th-century four-storey house. The large cellar that extends below the whole house is thought to have been used as a warehouse. It is also reputed to have been a gamekeeper's lodge for Windsor Park.

21. The Wokingham Wesleyan Orchestra, photographed in the 1920s.

22. The Westende and the Queen Victoria almshouses in the 1950s. The single-storey almshouses originated as the gift of John Westende in 1451. The others were built in 1887 and named in honour of Queen Victoria. All were demolished in 1978 and replaced by the Westende House and Queen Victoria House flats.

23. The Queen Victoria House flats under construction in 1980.

24 The Overhangs in Peach Street: a group of 15th-century buildings which are thought to have been associated with the Verderers' Courts of Windsor Forest. Over the years they degenerated to the condition shown in this photograph, taken in 1953. Fortunately, local pressure resulted in their restoration, and they are now in commercial use.

25. The Overhangs after they had been restored in 1970.

26.   Manny Rose, the chimney sweep, a well-known figure in the town, who lived with his family in Rose Street. This photograph shows him in Easthampstead Road about 1958.

27.   The Old Smithy was certainly here in Peach Street during the 1820s, and possibly earlier. This photograph, taken in 1980, shows it in use as a secondhand furniture shop. It has recently been renovated and is now used as the reception area for a new office development.

28.   These cottages in South Place were originally built as a silk factory in the 18th century. The factory was converted to a row of terraced houses after the industry collapsed in 1831. In spite of protests, they were demolished in 1980 to make way for an office block on the site.

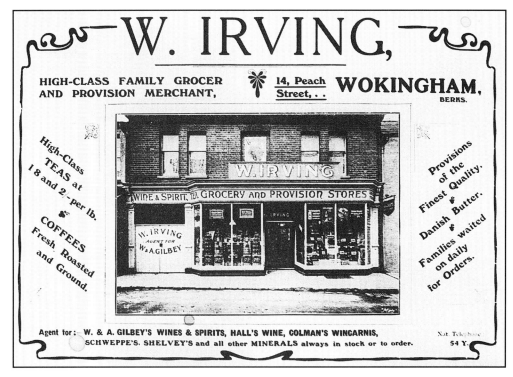

29. For about 30 years W. Irving had a grocer's shop at No. 14 Peach Street. He was one of a number of grocers in the town who also held a wines and spirits licence. In 1960 all that part of Peach Street was replaced by the present row of pre-cast concrete buildings.

30. Peach Street in the 1920s, looking east towards the Queen Victoria Almshouses in the distance. The *Redan* public house is on the left and still stands but, two houses further away on the same side of the road, the 18th-century *New Rose Inn* has now disappeared.

31. Somerscales supplied fish and chips from this shop in Peach Street, next to the *Redan* public house, both before and after the Second World War. It is still a fish and chip shop today.

32. Mr. Evans outside his leather shop at No. 19 Peach Street in 1905. He traded here from 1863 to 1918. His companions in the aprons are Mr. Lovelock, on the left, and Charlie Rideout, who was killed in the 1914-18 war, on the right.

33. By 1907 cycle dealers in Wokingham were already catering for the growing luxury market of the motor car. Note the hire purchase facilities and the discount for cash on bicycles in this advertisement for the Wokingham Motor & Cycle Works which had premises in Market Place and Peach Street.

Wokingham Motor and Cycle Works.

We Handle The Best Goods only, and supply at Popular Prices.

2/6 a Week will secure you a NEW HUDSON, TRIUMPH, PREMIER, B.S.A., EADIE, or ENFIELD CYCLE. Or if you pay Spot Cash a generous discount of 2/- in the Pound will be given you off List Prices.

The Most Up-to-date Shop for Cyclealities or Motoralities.

Every Machine has a Written Guarantee.

CALL, WRITE, OR PHONE!

WOKINGHAM MOTOR AND ::: CYCLE WORKS. :::

Telephone No. 55y.

Motor Pit & Garage: 11, Market Place
Showroom: 11, Peach Street.

34. The Market Place as it was in 1832. The Market House (Town Hall) depicted in this drawing was demolished in 1858 to make way for the present building. The area by the tree behind the Town Hall was the site of the notorious bull baiting. The last bull baiting in England took place here in 1852, despite a ban by the Wokingham Corporation in 1821 and the Act of 1827 banning this inhumane treatment of cattle.

35. The annual bull baiting in the Market Place. In Wokingham this 'sport' was endowed through the generosity of a local butcher, George Staverton, in 1661. He bequeathed a house, the rent from which (about £6) was to provide a bull for baiting on St Thomas' Day (21 December).

36. Traditional ox-roasting in the Market Place, one of the celebrations following the coronation of Queen Elizabeth II in 1953. The roasting began at 2 a.m. on Saturday 6 June, and slices of meat were distributed free of charge that afternoon.

37. This drawing was made in 1845, when Queen Victoria passed through Wokingham on her way to visit the Duke of Wellington at Stratfield Saye. The scene depicts Alderman Thomas Creaker presenting a loyal address to the queen.

38. Wokingham Town Hall at the turn of the century. This, the present Town Hall, was opened in 1860 by the high steward, Lord Braybrook. It also housed the police court and prison. The legend 'County Police Station' survives to the present day, high up on the north-west side of the building.

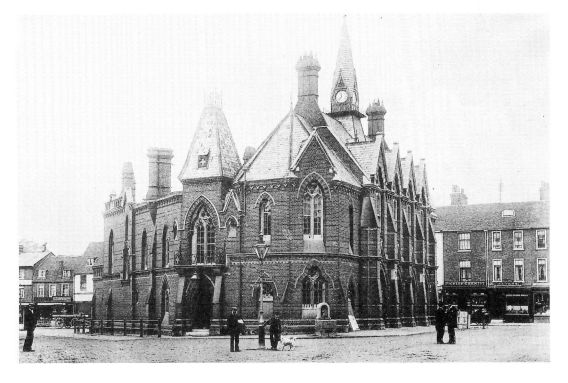

39.   Dr. F. S. M. Macphail presenting a copy of the Wokingham Market Charter of 1227 to Bob Naish, the mayor of Wokingham, in 1980.

40.   In the early 1900s the declaration of an election result from the balcony of the Town Hall attracted a much larger crowd than it would today.

41.   The Town Hall in the mid-1920s when the horse-drawn milk float was a common sight. The ornamental brickwork of the Town Hall is clearly visible. John Eighteen was the fishmonger at No. 40 Market Place for many years.

42. A corner of the Market Place in about 1925. The drinking trough, dated 1881, still survives despite a few accidents. The Thames Valley Traction Company began a regular and frequent bus service through Wokingham at this time. It is thought that the guests at the *Bush Hotel* complained that the passengers on the upper decks of the buses could look straight into their first-floor rooms, and petitioned for the bus stop to be moved along the road. It was certainly moved, though whether the petition influenced the decision is open to question.

43.   The timber-framed 15th- and 16th-century buildings that make up much of present-day Bush Walk were previously part of the *Bush Inn*. After being a stage coach inn for nearly 100 years, by the early 1900s when this photograph was taken it had become an hotel.

44. The Heelas shop in Market Place as it was about 1900.

45. Heelas, Wokingham's only department store. The Heelas family came to Wokingham from London in the 1790s and set up as shopkeepers. Their enterprise prospered, and by 1950 it occupied most of the north side of Market Place. One building remains as part of Boot's, but most was demolished and redeveloped in the late 1960s.

46.   This corner site of Rose Street and Market Place has a long history. As a timber-framed building it was the *Bell Inn* for about 100 years, up to about 1706. Then, through many alterations, it was a series of individual shops until it finally became part of the Heelas department store. It was demolished in the late 1960s.

47.   One of the last meetings of the Royal Buckhounds in the Market Place. This hunt had existed since the 18th century, but was eventually abolished in 1901. The Boxing Day meet of the Garth Hunt continued until the early 1960s.

48. The Conservative Committee rooms in Gotelee House, Market Place, during the General Election of 1885. The successful candidate was Sir George Russell, who lived at Swallowfield Park. He was M.P. for East Berkshire, which included Wokingham. Gotelee House is a mid-18th-century town house with bow-fronted windows, which now houses the Halifax Building Society.

49. Built in the 18th century, this building at No. 11 Market Place has been put to many uses. During this century alone, the site was used as a garage up to 1910, a wire rope works in the early 1920s, became The Coffee House in the 1930s, and today is easily recognised as Dorothy Perkins' shop.

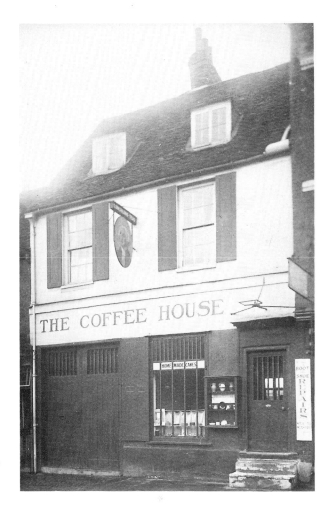

50. During the 1939-45 war, the Market Place was a very convenient assembly point for troops. This time it was the turn of the Home Guard to assemble for an exercise.

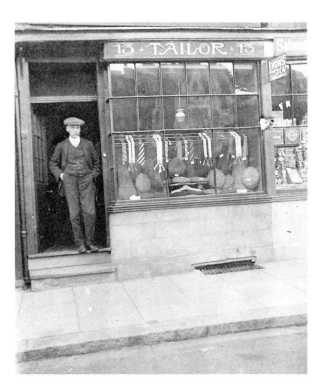

51. Mr. Albert Goswell, tailor, outside his shop at No. 13 Market Place. For over 40 years he carried on his business there, specialising in hunt and livery clothing. He was also a very keen member of the Wokingham fire brigade, serving for nearly 40 years and rising to the rank of lieutenant.

52. This photograph of 1900 shows the house in Denmark Street where the *Wokingham Times* was first produced. For many years, under different names, it was a grocery. It has now been rebuilt and houses the kitchen shop, Carpenters.

53. The entrance to the Drill Hall photographed in the early 1970s. The Drill Hall was built by Arthur Walter in 1881 and was used for dances, meetings and, above all, by the Territorial Army.

54. This view from inside the forecourt of the Drill Hall was taken in the mid-1970s before the hall was demolished to make way for the shopping precinct in Erftstadt Court.

55. The Wellington Brewery was closed in the 1920s. In the 1970s the brewery buildings housed the Berkshire Craft Centre and this photograph shows them in 1975, a few years before demolition.

56. Denmark Street in the early 1900s. The gabled building on the left dates from the 17th century and much of its timber frame is still visible from the interior. The cottages beyond, now demolished, once housed a chimney sweep and a boot repairer.

57. The *Duke's Head*, *c.*1895. Originally three cottages, it was first mentioned as a public house in 1795. The two entrance doors shown in this photograph have now been blocked up and a modern entrance has been made on the left of the building. The yard of the present public house contains a 200-year-old building, now restored for use as a skittle alley.

58. Jack and Pip Trill's cycle shop was a well-known landmark in Denmark Street until it closed down in the 1970s. Many in the town bought their bicycles there.

59.   It would be unthinkable for a coach to pick up passengers in Denmark Street today. Sadly, the *Royal Exchange* was demolished in 1962.

60.   This shop at No. 2 Denmark Street was run by Elizabeth and Len Freeman. It was formerly the studio of Mr. Brant, a well-known photographer in the town.

61. No. 7 Market Place, which stands between the *Roebuck* and Gotelee House, was a popular sweet shop run by Harry 'Frump' Hawkins of a long-established Wokingham family.

62. Denmark Street looking towards Market Place as it was in the 1950s, showing no sign of the changes to come. On the left is the entrance to the Drill Hall, and on the right are Exchange Cottages, so called after the nearby public house.

63. A view from Market Place looking down into Denmark Street, c.1913. The *Wheatsheaf Inn* is an early 19th-century building which is now occupied by Oddbins.

64.   A horse and caravan, 'Traveller' and 'Bullrush', standing outside Nos. 21-22 Market Place in 1911. The last horse and van disappeared from Wokingham several years ago, and these buildings have been demolished, too.

65.   Red Lion Passage photographed in the 1960s, running between the *Red Lion* on the right and the now demolished Sale's shop, which was formerly the *King's Head Inn*.

66. Red Lion Passage on a sunny day in the 1960s, showing the rear of the *Red Lion*. The steeply pitched roofs are those of two 15th- and 16th-century buildings which originally had thatched roofs.

67. The demolition in 1977 of No. 26 Market Place, once the *King's Head Inn*. This was a fine 16th-century building similar to the *Red Lion*, the rear of which can just be seen on the left of the picture. The site is now occupied by W. H. Smith and the Abbey National.

68.   The Peace Day celebrations on 22 July 1919. This is a general view of the Market Place during the celebrations, showing the *Wheatsheaf Inn*, Goswell the Tailors, Cope's grocery, John Lapper and Son, pork butchers, and Thimbleby and Shorland, auctioneers. Cattle, sheep and pigs were sold in the Market Place at weekly markets.

W. CHAMBERS

Caterer, Baker, Cook and Confectioner.

Balls, Suppers and Wedding Receptions on the shortest notice.

Ices, Jellies and Creams to Order.

Plate, Linen, Glass, Tables, &c., on Hire.

Wine, Ale & Beer Merchant.

Bass & Co.'s, Ind Coope & Co.s, and Simond's Ales and Stout,

In Cask, Bottle, and on Draught.

Foreign and British Wines.

MARKET PLACE, WOKINGHAM.

69. Wokingham has always been well supplied with bakers and confectioners. William Chambers had his shop at No. 4 Market Place in the early 1900s and, like many other bakers and confectioners, he also sold beers, wines and spirits.

70. The Market Place, looking towards Denmark Street about the turn of the century. On the left is the *Rose Hotel* and Butler's grocery. Note the gravel road surface and the lack of traffic.

71.   The *Rose Hotel* was once two buildings to which the licence of the original *Rose Inn* was transferred in the mid-19th century. It has been one of the centres of Wokingham life ever since. It was renamed *Ye Olde Rose Inne* in 1923, shortly after this photograph was taken.

72.   Older residents of the town will recognise the scene in the Market Place in the 1950s. The shop of Hussey and Son has long since gone and Boot's has moved to larger premises nearby.

73.   The proclamation of King George V in 1910 outside the Town Hall attracted a very large crowd, with some risk to those who chose the best vantage points from which to hear the announcement.

74.   When one of the Heelas buildings in the centre of the town caught fire it provided a dramatic subject for an enterprising photographer. In view of the many adjoining timber-framed buildings, prompt action was needed to avert a major fire.

75.   The scene after the debris had been removed shows that the upper storey of the building was completely destroyed.

T. MARIS,

Saddler and Harness Maker,

Horses carefully Measured and Neatly Fitted.

GENERAL REPAIRS.

London Whips,	Rope, Twine,
Bits and Spurs,	Oils, and
Horse Clothing, &c.,	Cart Grease.

Market Place, Wokingham.

76. Peach Street and part of Market Place in the 1960s. David Greig at No. 33 Market Place is now occupied by Bejam. It was formerly occupied by Colebrook's, the butchers, who used to purchase the prize-winning bulls at local shows and exhibit their heads complete with rosettes in their window. Their abattoir was at the rear in Luckley Path.

77. The traditional leather industry of Wokingham meant there were always several saddlers and harness makers in the town. This advertisement for T. Maris shows one that, in the last years of the 19th century, had a shop in Market Place on part of the site where Milwards now stands.

78.   Broad Street in 1914. There have been fewer changes here than in many other parts of the town, though some trees have gone, some buildings have been pulled down and rebuilt, and the traffic island in the middle of the road has been extended towards Shute End.

79.   Broad Street in the late 1890s, looking towards Tudor House. The road was still surfaced with gravel and the end of Rose Street, then called Row Lane, had now been widened. The bollard blocking the narrow entrance to Row Lane, and the shop that was pulled down when the widening took place, can be seen to the left of the man on horseback.

80. The junction of Rose Street and Broad Street in the early 1960s. The shop on the corner was a café and cake shop well known to the inhabitants of the town. It was an old timber-framed building called the *George Inn* during the early part of the 17th century.

81. Broad Street, about the turn of the century, looking towards Shute End. The gas lamps, the gravel road surface and the few pedestrians all evoke a bygone age. The far end of the street was mostly residential and the end nearer Market Place consisted mainly of shops.

82. By 1915 more shops had appeared at the Market Place end of Broad Street. The town's first cinema, the Electric Theatre, opened a few years earlier.

83.   The Elms, in Broad Street, about 1970. The original house, built in the 15th century, was completely enclosed by the 18th-century structure seen today. At one time it was the Dower House to the Swallowfield Estate. It was bought by the Ellison family in 1892.

84.   The old Wokingham post office at the turn of the century. The site was bought by the Westminster Bank and was in use as their Wokingham branch until the 1980s. The present National Westminster Bank building occupies the whole of this corner site.

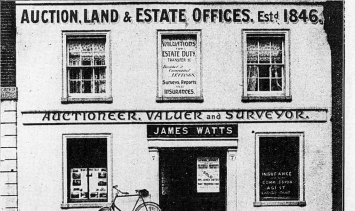

JAMES WATTS,

Auctioneer, Valuer & Surveyor, Land, House & Estate Agent,

INSURANCES EFFECTED.

7, Broad Street, WOKINGHAM, Berks.

Auction Sales of all kinds.

Valuations and Surveys.

Land, House, and Estate Agent. &c.

Plans.
Inventories.

AUCTION, LAND & ESTATE OFFICES. Estd 1846.

VALUATIONS FOR ESTATE DUTY. TRANSFER &c.

Business & Commercial LETTINGS.

Surveys, Reports AND INSURANCES.

AUCTIONEER, VALUER and SURVEYOR.

JAMES WATTS

INSURANCE & COMMISSION AGENT

AGENCY

Particulars of Properties Free on Application.—

INVENTORIES taken and checked.

ESTATES MANAGED.

Accounts Audited. Rents Collected.

Land, Estates, Houses, and Businesses required in all parts.

VALUATIONS

for
PROBATE & ESTATE DUTY.
PARTNERSHIP.
BUSINESS TRANSFER.
TIMBER.
TENANT RIGHT.
MORTGAGE.

AUCTIONS

of
Freehold, Leasehold,
or
Copyhold Properties.
FURNITURE.
Silver. Works of Art.
Reversionary Interests.
Life Policies,
FARM SALES, Etc.

INSURANCES

FIRE, LIFE, ACCIDENT.
Employers' Liability.
Domestic Servants.
Burglary,
Larceny or Theft,
Plate Glass. Live Stock.

Prospectus FREE.

ADVICE GRATIS!! NO CHARGE unless Business Results.   Address:—

Mr. JAMES WATTS, Auctioneer, Valuer & Surveyor, WOKINGHAM.

85.   An advertisement for an estate agent in Wokingham in the late 19th century. The 17th-century house has been used as estate agents' offices for nearly 150 years. Martin and Pole are the current occupiers.

86. Residential sites and industry side by side in Broad Street before 1914. The Wokingham Brewery closed down early in the 1914-18 war and a block of offices was recently built on the site. The building on the right now houses Astral Sports. In the 15th century there was a bell foundry at the rear of these premises.

87. The tranquil back garden of the house that is now Astral Sports, photographed about 1925.

PITHER & SON (Late HOLLIS)

Purveyors of
Home-killed English Meat of superior quality
at Strictly Moderate Prices.

GAME, FISH, POULTRY AND ICE.

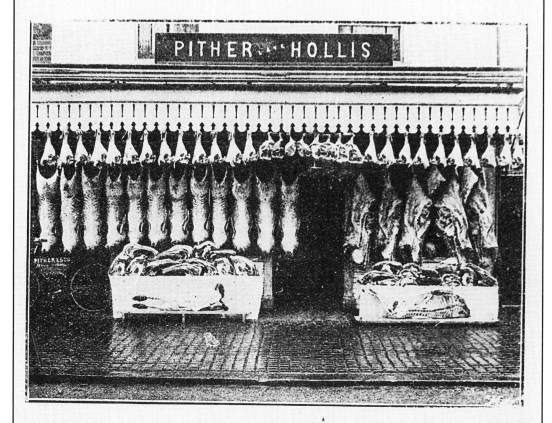

Personal and Prompt Attention to all Orders.

BROAD ST., WOKINGHAM.

BRANCHES:
SWALLOWFIELD AND SPENCER'S WOOD, SHINFIELD.

Established 1860.   Telephone—20, WOKINGHAM

88.   The Pither family were butchers in Wokingham as early as 1860. Although they no longer have a shop in Broad Street, their name can still be seen high up on the wall above the Halifax estate agency.

Paris House · 15^A BROAD ST · WOKINGHAM

WORK·SHOP

FITTING·ROOM

Ladies & Gentlemen's TAILOR

HUNTING SUITS & LIVERIES A Speciality

DRY CLEANING AND REPAIRS of all Descriptions

89.   Paris House in Broad Street has been put to many uses. Early in this century it was a bootmaker's. In the 1920s and 1930s it was a tailor's, as shown by this advertisement. Today it houses the offices of the Halifax estate agency.

90.   Montague House, *c.*1960. This house has had a long connection with education. In 1654 Henry Montague, a school master and non-conformist, ran a school there. In 1806 it was owned by John Roberts, a well-known Wokingham solicitor, and became a school again in 1920 when Grosvenor House School moved there. This school moved away in 1930 and Berkshire County Council bought the property in 1951. It now houses the Wokingham Library and the Adult Education Centre.

91. This earliest known photograph of Wokingham in the late 1850s shows an obviously posed group of people in Broad Street. The houses on the left still survive with their frontages little altered, but the warehouse and the large tree that masks Montague House have now gone.

92.   Broad Street in 1924, viewed from the west, presented a peaceful vista, far removed from the present-day scene with its constant stream of traffic. Apart from the loss of most of the attractive trees, the street itself appears to have changed very little.

93.   The former Perkin's garage at the west end of Broad Street in the 1920s, with a magnificent display of the latest models from the Morris company. The cottages have since been pulled down and were replaced by a modern garage. This has in turn been replaced by a new office block, called Rectory Court.

94. In 1919 the Grosvenor School for Girls occupied what is now called Tudor House. This 16th-century building formed an imposing end to Broad Street.

95. During the 1920s the timber façade from a demolished building at Binfield was attached to Tudor House. It can be seen in this 1950s' photograph and has been retained to the present day. The house, therefore, gives the impression of being unchanged since it was first built as a 'mansion' in the late 16th century.

96. A winter scene in Milton Road about 1902. This part of the road is now completely built up, though the far end has not been so heavily developed.

97. Martin's Pool in 1935. William Thomas Martin built this open-air swimming pool at his own expense and first opened it to the public in 1934. He sold the pool to Wokingham Borough Council in 1946, and it is still in public use.

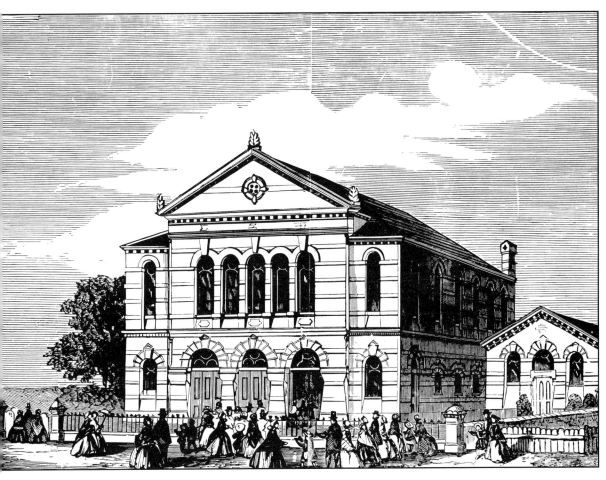

98.   An early print of the Baptist chapel in Milton Road which was built in 1864 to replace a smaller chapel.

99. In 1910 only a single car gives any hint of what the traffic would be like at the western end of Broad Street in the 1990s
The 16th-century Tudor House, then Grosvenor School and with ivy-covered render instead of the present Tudor façade,
dominated the area as it still does today.

100. This view from Broad Street into Shute End, taken about 1900, shows an old three-storey house on the right, once
called Terrace Point. It later became Grosvenor School and is now known as Tudor House. On the left, at the beginning
of Shute End, is Mr. W. H. Howard's ironmongery. In the distance can be seen St Paul's Elementary School.

101. Shute End in 1859, with the subjects of the photograph carefully posing for the new-fangled camera. St Paul's Elementary School, Parish Room and Clock Tower were not yet built, but the *Hope and Anchor* was already there.

102.   The spire of St Paul's church can be seen in the background of this photograph of The Terrace taken about 1880. Note the double row of chain on the railings. The houses shown on the corner of Station Road and Reading Road were demolished in 1893 to make way for the Parish Room and Clock Tower.

103.   The sign by the parked car welcomes careful motorists to Wokingham in this photograph of Shute End taken in the late 1920s or early 1930s. Perhaps the lady had been calling at St Paul's Rectory or on Admiral Eustace, a near neighbour in Admiral House, both just to the left of this viewpoint. The Rectory has recently been considerably extended to become the main offices of the Wokingham District Council.

The Terrace – Wokingham

104. By the end of 1894 St Paul's Elementary School, Parish Room and Clock Tower had all been erected at the expense of John Walter III. The tower is 42 ft. high and the clock strikes on a bell weighing 7 cwt. The buildings were purchased and presented to the parish of St Paul's by Thomas Edward Ellison in March 1911. The post and chain fence around the triangle of grass seen in the centre of the picture was removed in 1940 as part of the war effort.

105. August 1908: the lower end of The Terrace looking towards Reading has a distinctive Edwardian elegance about it, with painted railings, and children being taken for a summer walk.

106.   This view along the Reading Road, looking towards the town, shows the beginning of The Terrace. The signpost indicates the road to Barkham and the railway station.

107.   Station Road in 1910, looking up the hill towards The Terrace from the railway crossing. The prestigious *Railway Hotel* has now become the *Molly Millar*. Hosler's ironmongery, on the right, closed down in 1989. Contemporary newspaper reports deplored the traffic hold-ups caused by the level crossing.

108. The *Hope and Anchor* still occupies this 15th-century hall-house at the top of Station Road. In 1907, at the time of this photograph, it was owned by Baker, Powell and Co., the Wokingham Brewery which was based in Broad Street. John Capon was then landlord. Barker and Sons, next door, were shoeing smiths.

109. Wokingham railway station as it looked about 1910. The footbridge was constructed from lengths of old railway line, and is still in constant use. The railway came to Wokingham in 1849 when the Reading to Guildford line was opened. The direct route to London opened later when the Reading to Staines line was built under the Staines, Wokingham and Woking Junction Railway Act.

110. The large marshalling yard at Wokingham station in the 1920s, all under snow. The Station Industrial Estate now occupies much of the marshalling yard to the right of the main line and car parking has taken over the rest.

111. Ten staff of Wokingham railway station at the end of the 19th century. Note the large enamelled panel advertisements which were a feature of the station well into the middle of this century. Minchin Brothers were a local firm of corn, coal, hay, seed, straw and oilcake merchants, forage contractors and brick and tile manufacturers.

112.   The Wokingham Union Workhouse was built in Barkham Road in 1850 to replace the older workhouse in Denmark Street. It became an emergency hospital in 1939 and the Wokingham Hospital in 1948. Until recently it still catered for maternity needs, and even now maintains wards for geriatric cases.

113.   This photograph of the interior of the workhouse in Barkham Road shows the very spartan conditions prevailing at the turn of the century. The photograph also captures the spirit of the times with the message of congratulations to Lord Roberts, the commander of the British forces towards the end of the Boer War.

114. Barkham Road was a quiet tree-lined road in 1915, before the development of our present-day housing estates.

115. The Tan House, off Barkham Road, as it looked in the early years of this century. It was the last surviving site in Wokingham where leather was made and did not cease production until the 1920s. In the 19th century leather working and the manufacture of boots and shoes were the main industries in the town.

116. Folly Court, as it was in 1977, before it was demolished to make way for the training centre for guide dogs for the blind. Built during the second half of the 19th century, it was the home of several prominent local families. Sale and Son, the local seedsmen, also used it as their head office for many years.

117. With the rapid expansion of the town, many shops that served their local community have now disappeared. One such was C. F. Belcher's butcher's shop, which for more than 30 years from the 1930s served the Evendons area. Today the premises are occupied as a private house.

118. One of the most attractive roads in the district, Wellingtonia Avenue, was built in the 1870s by John Walter II, the owner of the *Times* newspaper, and planted with Wellingtonia sequoia trees as a memorial to the Duke of Wellington. At the beginning of this century when this photograph was taken, the trees were still only part grown and gave no real indication of their present impressive appearance.

119. Bearwood was built by John Walter III in the 1860s. During the 1914-18 war it was used as a convalescent hospital for Canadian servicemen. After the war it was sold by the Walter family and became an orphanage and training school for the children of merchant seamen. It now houses Bearwood College (R.M.N.S.), an independent day and boarding school for boys.

120. In the 1920s the Loddon still flowed almost entirely through open country and the bridge over it, now part of the A329, was quiet and peaceful.

121. The road from Reading to Wokingham in about 1917 was a wide but muddy track which was full of pot-holes. This scene shows the *Pheasant* standing almost in isolation and hardly recognisable as the well-known public house of today.

122.   This scene was captured in the grounds of Toutley Hall around the turn of the century. Cars were very new and fashionable then, and the driver was obviously very proud of his vehicle.

123.   In the early 1920s the crossroads at Winnersh provided a quiet suburban scene, with a solitary car turning left. Only fragments of this scene remain today, perhaps the most prominent being the telegraph pole.

124.   The footbridge at Embrook shows that in 1914 the stream could rise and make the ford impassable for travellers on foot. Today this quiet country lane has become one of the main roads into Embrook and the stream is normally unnoticed by the traveller passing in a car.

The Ford
Embrook, nr Wokingham.   A.443.

125.   Embrook Stores, *c.*1920, during a promotion for Lipton's tea. The proprietor, Mr. Edward Farnell, is standing in the doorway with his son Eric, who died at the young age of eight years. Mr. Farnell was also the local sub-postmaster.

126. The *Dog and Duck* at Embrook started life as a beerhouse. Absolom Deane received the first licence in 1851 when he was 80 years old. By the time of this photograph, taken in the early years of this century, it was an attractive public house in a rural setting.

127. The peace and quiet of this scene by the *Rifle Volunteer* on the Reading Road about 1910 has vanished for ever, leaving only the public house as a reminder of times past. Today the heavy traffic, the minor industrial estate behind the public house and the nearby Woosehill roundabout demonstrate how much the scene has changed.

28. St Paul's church was built entirely at the expense
of John Walter III and was consecrated on 23 July
1864. The church has changed little, as shown by this
photograph taken about 1900.

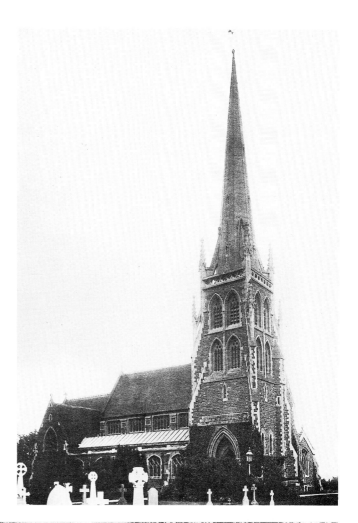

29. The lovely tree-lined approach to Wokingham
along the Reading Road. Sadly, most of these trees
succumbed to Dutch Elm disease.

130. Beches Manor is thought to have been named after Roger de la Beche, who owned large estates in Berkshire in the 15th century. This building was dated 1624 over the main entrance. By 1840 it was the home of James Hayward, who also owned the Wokingham Brewery and all but two of the public houses in Wokingham at that time. After the Hayward Estate was sold in 1856, the house had a succession of owners, finally becoming an hotel, which was destroyed by fire in 1953.

131. This building, now the Holt School, was almost certainly the Dower House attached to Beches Manor. On the death in 1729 of Richard Hawes, the owner of Beches Manor, the Holt passed into separate ownership, and a number of prominent Wokingham families have since owned it. In 1885 the house passed from the Crutchley family to the Heelas family, whose additions and alterations gave the house its present appearance. Berkshire County Council acquired the house in 1930 and opened it as the Holt County School for Girls in 1931.

132. Although there has been a house on this Matthews Green site since the 14th century, the present house named Cantley was built in 1880. The property of over 100 acres with all its buildings was acquired by the Wokingham District Council in 1976. Sports pitches were opened in 1980, and since then facilities have been gradually expanded. The house is now leased out and run as an hotel and country club.

133. Glebelands, a private house designed by Ernest Newton R.A., was built in 1897. In 1936 it was bought and given to the Cinematograph Trade Benevolent Fund as a rest and convalescent home. Much expanded over the years, today it still provides peace and quiet for up to 30 residents.

134.   The Palmer Schools, built in 1875 as the last of a succession of schools created with the charitable bequests of Dr. Palmer in 1711 and of Martha Palmer in 1713. The photograph was taken in 1976, not long before the schools were demolished and replaced by Meachen Court as sheltered accommodation for the elderly.

135.   High Close, built around 1895, was originally a private house off Wiltshire Road which had extensive grounds. It was bought by Barnardo's and in the 1980s, after many alterations and an opening by Cliff Richard, became home to 48 youngsters aged between 9 and 16, all housed in small family units.

136. This stone was erected on the Forest Road at Bill Hill to commemorate the upgrading of the road in about 1770 into one fit for stage coaches. Although the cost was met by private subscription and for many years the road was one of the coach routes from Reading to London, there is no known record of it being a turnpike.

137. Buckhurst House on the London Road is now known as Stakis St Anne's Manor. It was originally the home of William Heelas and later that of Charles Townsend Murdoch, one time M.P. for Reading. In 1939 Buckhurst House became St Anne's Nursing and Convalesent Home which was run by a nursing order of nuns.

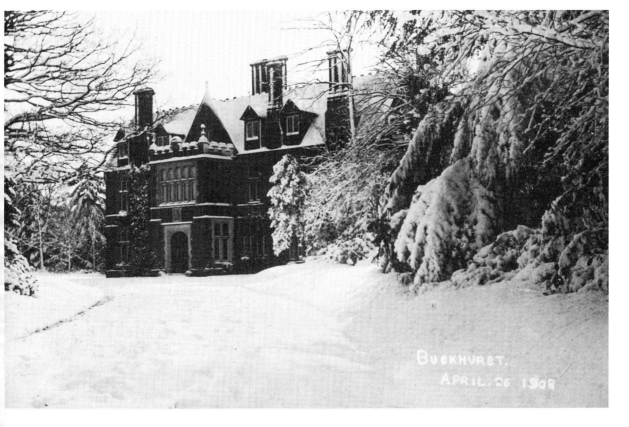

138.   About the beginning of this century Wokingham was starting to expand along London Road towards Bracknell. As this picture shows, however, less than 400 yards from All Saints' church the road was still part of a quiet country scene.

139.   Red Lodge was typical of some of the early buildings along London Road near St Crispin's School. This photograph shows it in about 1909.

140. The first stages in the modern expansion of Wokingham on its eastern boundaries. This aerial view, taken about 1960, shows an incomplete Norreys estate with Keephatch Road on the far edge of the estate and Ashridge Road in the foreground.

141. Easthampstead Mansion, the home of the Marquis of Downshire, was at the height of its fame at the beginning of this century. In the 1939-45 war, half of the house was occupied by St Paul's School from London. The house was later bought by Berkshire County Council and is now an educational centre.

142. The Wokingham and District Agricultural Show was inaugurated in 1835 and has since been held annually on various farms around the area. Since 1985 it has settled at Whitehouse Farm, in Spencers Wood, and is now named the Wokingham and Reading Agricultural Show.

143.   A shooting party of local businessmen on the Billingbear Estate. From left to right: T. B. Pither, H. Bowyer, S. Brewin (gamekeeper), A. E. Bullock, W. B. Martin, W. S. Medcalf. A very good 'bag' for the day.

144. The *White Horse*, pictured in 1939, has existed since at least 1848. The original public house was replaced by the present building in 1860 to bring it closer to the road.

145. Starmead was one of a series of large houses in Wokingham designed by Joseph Morris. It was built in the late 19th century on a large plot in Easthampstead Road. In the 1970s it was replaced by the present small housing estate bounded by Starmead Drive.

146. In the early years of this century the far end of Easthampstead Road was little more than a country lane with the large houses of Mertonford and Starmead near the junction with Murdoch Road.

147. Before the 1914-18 war this scene in Easthampstead Road, with its gas lamps and horse droppings, was typical of most roads in Wokingham at that time. The prominent building on the left is All Saints' Church House.

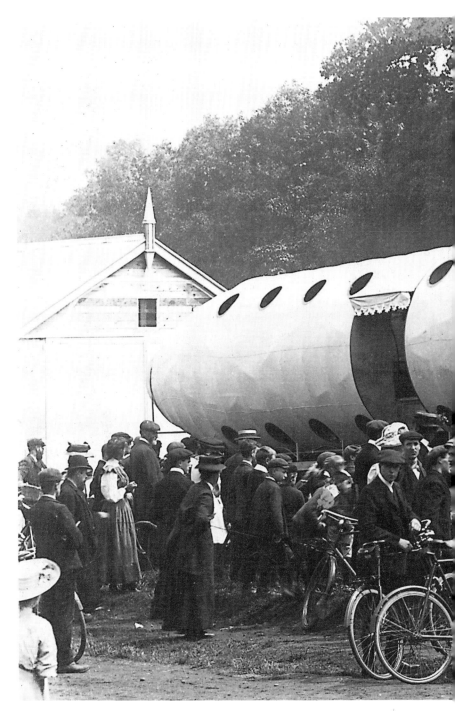

148. Jesse Farbrother of Wescott Road designed, patented and built the 'Wokingham Whale' in Easthampstead Road. This photograph shows the 60-ft. long by 14-ft. wide and 16-ft. high fuselage of the aircraft being taken to Windsor in 1909 to have an 80-h.p. engine with 1,200-r.p.m. propeller fitted. Not surprisingly, it never flew.

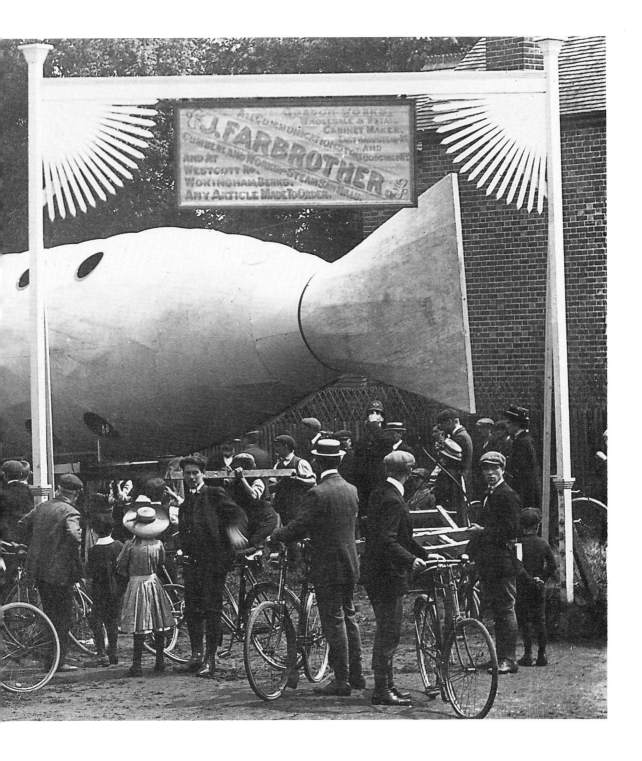

149. Unlike today, in 1929 there were many small shops in Wokingham. J. Jordinson's, the greengrocery at No. 7 Easthampstead Road, was well known. Today the building is used as an art gallery.

150. In 1910 Nine Mile Ride was just that – a very pleasant track for a ride or ramble.

151. In the early years of this century Wixenford School claimed to be a 'school for the sons of gentlemen and minor princes'. Although the name has since been changed to Ludgrove, it has continued as a school and now has Prince William as a pupil.

152. This former lodge to the Wixenford Estate, seen here about 1916, still exists although much altered, and can be found at the end of Luckley Road.

The Entrance,
Wixenford, Wokingham.
A.927

153. In 1663 Henry Lucas bequeathed £7,000 to provide a hospital as a home for 16 old men from the 32 neighbouring parishes, of which half were in Berkshire and the rest in Surrey. This magnificent building is the only Grade I listed building in Wokingham.

154. Four residents sunning themselves outside the Lucas Hospital in the 1880s.

155. The former lodge on the Luckley Estate, photographed about 1930, still stands guard on the corner of Luckley Road and Finchampstead Road.

156. There was little trouble with traffic at East Heath on the Finchampstead Road in 1915. One could have a pleasant walk along this gravel-surfaced road in the summer but it would become very rutted in the winter.

157.   The approach to Wokingham along the Finchampstead Road has changed a great deal since the beginning of this century and now there are houses on both sides of the road.

158.   This terrace of houses at Nos. 46-52 Finchampstead Road was built between Carey Road and the railway bridge, in two stages during the 1860s and the 1870s, on what had previously been a brickfield. They were demolished in 1989 and the site is being used for yet another office building.

159. This single cottage stood at the end of Cockpit Path on what is now part of the *Olde Rose Inne* car park. The cottáge was demolished about 1960.

160. Langborough recreation ground at the beginning of this century. The large houses in Fairview Road were newly built and the row of lime trees was newly planted. The houses are still there, as is the recreation ground. The limes have matured into a magnificent row of trees.

161. The Peace Day celebrations in 1919 on Langborough recreation ground where the steam fire engine was being used to roast the potatoes.

162. This aerial photograph, taken in the early 1970s, shows the centre of Wokingham. Even though large areas of the town have been redeveloped, the main road layout from earlier times is still intact.

163.   These two cottages in Luckley Path are pictured here in 1965, a few years before they were demolished. At the far end were the stables where the Co-operative Stores kept the horses for their delivery carts.

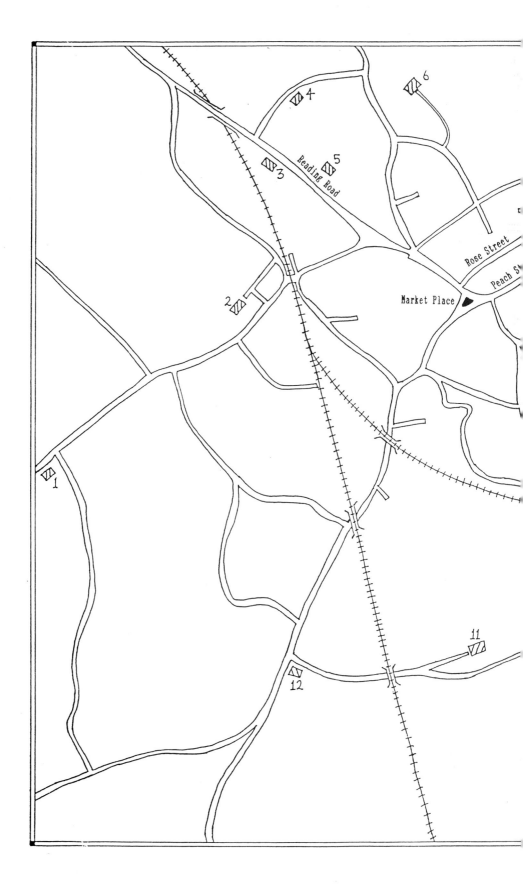